S0-AFF-538

NOT FOR CIRCULATION

TRACTORS, PLOWS, AND HARVESTERS

ROSEMONT SCHOOL LIBRARY

NORMAN RICHARDS

TRACTORS, PLOWS, and HARVESTERS

A Book About Farm Machines

DOUBLEDAY & COMPANY, INC. GARDEN CITY, NEW YORK

631.3
Ri

PHOTO CREDITS

Allis-Chalmers, pp. 13, 24, 32, 36, 41, 42, 45
Case, p. 14
International Harvester, pp. 11, 17, 20, 22, 26, 31, 49, 50, 53, 54
John Deere, pp. 19, 28, 35, 38, 46, 57, 59

This book is part of a Museum of Science and Industry/Chicago series of science books published by Doubleday & Company, Inc. The series is designed to inform, stimulate, and challenge youngsters on a wide range of scientific and technological subjects.

Library of Congress Cataloging in Publication Data

Richards, Norman.
  Tractors, plows, and harvesters.

  (Chicago's Museum of Science and Industry/Doubleday
books)
  SUMMARY: Photographs with captions identify modern
farm machinery.
  1. Agricultural machinery—Juvenile literature.
[1. Agricultural machinery] I. Title. II. Series.
S675.R49   631.3
ISBN 0-385-12347-7 Trade
      0-385-12348-5 Prebound
Library of Congress Catalog Card Number 77–83821

Copyright © 1978 by Norman V. Richards
All rights reserved
Printed in the United States of America
First Edition

ROSEMONT SCHOOL LIBRARY

6257

This book is
dedicated to
TROY

PREFACE

This book is about some wonderful machines that have changed the lives of farmers in the United States and many other countries.

Only fifty years ago, more than one third of the American people lived on farms and struggled to raise enough food for the country. Farming was hard, slow work, and most of it was done by hand. A farmer could plow only a single row at a time, walking behind a plow pulled by a horse. He cut his grain with a scythe and picked his vegetables by hand. He used a pitchfork to load hay into a horse-drawn wagon. With these slow methods, each farm worker could produce only a small amount of crops each year.

But then came the inventions of all sorts of farm machines, which did much of the hard work in plowing, planting, cultivating, and harvesting. With these machines, and with greater scientific knowledge of agriculture, each farmer is able to produce many times the amount of crops he could fifty years ago. Today, only 2 per cent of the American people work in agriculture, yet they raise more than enough food for the entire country. Farmers have made similar progress in other countries. And it's largely because of the fascinating machines shown in this book.

N.R.

TRACTORS, PLOWS, AND HARVESTERS

This is how farmers cut their grain a hundred years ago. It was hard, slow work in the hot sun. Three men could harvest only two acres of grain in a day. It wasn't much fun.

Today, farmers use big machines like this one to harvest their crops. One person operates the machine. He sits in the driver's seat behind the big window and stays cool, because the cab is air-conditioned. Big blades in front whirl around and cut the grain. A machine like this one can harvest nearly one hundred acres a day.

Machines are used in every stage of growing crops. Before seeds are planted, a farmer must break up the ground with a plow. This allows air and water to reach the seeds in the earth so they can grow. This machine plows in wide rows to save time.

The rough, plowed soil is cultivated next. This means it is smoothed and leveled with a cultivator, sometimes called a harrow. Small, circular blades, or disks, loosen the topsoil so seeds can be planted. While the machine is doing its work, the farmer can drive and listen to the radio in his tractor.

What is this strange-looking machine? It's another cultivator. Some of them are too wide to pull over the roads to farm fields. So they are specially made to fold up when traveling on roads. The tall parts will fold down in the field to cultivate wide areas.

Now that his fields have been plowed and cultivated, this farmer is going to plant soybean seeds with a machine called a planter. He fills the machine's tanks with seeds. He can also put fertilizer in some tanks.

The seeds and fertilizer are dropped by the machine in rows, allowing the right amount of space needed for each plant to grow. The fertilizer enriches the soil and "feeds" the plants, helping them to grow stronger and faster.

Some farmers use a method called double cropping. While a machine called a harvester gathers ripe soybeans, a tractor and planter follow close behind, planting another crop. The farmer doesn't plow the field, because the ground is still soft from plowing for the first crop. This saves time and work.

ROSEMONT SCHOOL LIBRARY

6257

Cultivators are also used to dig up weeds and loosen soil while crops are growing. Weeds use too much water and fertilized soil while they are growing. This doesn't leave enough to help these young corn plants grow, so the weeds are removed. The machine's digging blades are spaced to go between the rows so the corn plants won't be damaged.

This fancy machine has a 315-gallon tank for agricultural chemicals. The farmer uses it to spray special chemicals around vegetable plants. The chemicals drive insects away, keeping them from eating the vegetables.

Here is an easier and faster way to pick cotton. The farmer sits in his cool, air-conditioned cab and drives through the cotton fields. The machine pulls the fluffy, white cotton bolls from the stalks and stores them in the big container at the rear.

This farmer can harvest sorghum and other grains quickly with his combine harvester. It's called a combine because it does two things: it cuts and grinds the grain, and it has the power to drive itself—it doesn't have to be pulled by a tractor.

A different type of cutting head is used when a farmer harvests soybeans. The pointed "teeth" go between the rows of plants. This forces the plants into a grinder, which separates the beans. The beans are blown into the machine's storage tank.

34

Here is a combine harvester with an attachment for picking corn. This corn is used to feed cattle and hogs. The machine grinds the whole cornstalk and stores it in its tank.

Farmers used to work until sundown, but now they can work after dark, too. Many modern farm machines have bright lights on them.

It looks like a monster coming, but it's only a wheat-harvesting machine. The wide blades in front can cut large areas of wheat very quickly.

40

When the harvester's storage tank is full of ground-up wheat, farmers pour the grain into a truck through the tall pipe.

After the ground-up grain is poured into trucks, it is ready to be taken to a silo. It will be stored there. Later, it will be ground more finely into flour for baking, or it may be used as animal feed.

Special harvesting machines are made for working on hillsides.
The wheels and cutting blades tilt like the hillside, but the
driver stays level.

Four giant harvesters form a "caravan" to cut grain faster on a large western wheat farm. Farmers often work together, each with his own machine, helping each other.

It is easier to move hay and other crops from the fields if it is
made into bales. This baling machine makes large, round bales
very quickly. The bales are loaded onto trucks and taken
to a silo for storage.

Even on a small farm, a baling machine can save time and work. This small baler makes tight blocks of hay, which are carried on the wagon behind the tractor.

Some machines make tiny cubes of grain to be fed to cattle.
When the machine has made all the cubes it can hold, they are
dumped into a truck and taken to the cattle.

The little cubes look like this after the baling machine has packed the hay very tightly. They are easy to handle and do not take much space when they are stored.

And what a delicious meal they make for these hungry fellows!
Thanks to modern machines, today's farmers can grow more
food than ever before—for people and for animals.

Norman Richards lived on a small farm in New England as a child. When he was a teen-ager, he worked summers on farms where vegetables and hay were the main crops. "Anyone who has worked on a farm can appreciate the wonderful benefits of modern farm machines," he says.

Mr. Richards studied journalism at Boston University, where he received his bachelor of science degree, and did graduate work at Harvard University. He has been a magazine editor and writer for a number of years and has traveled throughout the world on writing assignments covering a wide variety of subjects.

He is also the author of eighteen previous books, including two Junior Literary Guild selections: THE STORY OF OLD IRONSIDES and GIANTS IN THE SKY, a book about dirigibles.

Mr. Richards lives in the country, at Wilton, Connecticut, not far from New York City.

ROSEMONT SCHOOL LIBRARY